An Unbreakable Bond
The Ultimate Mother & Daughter Relationship

by
Tracey Hines

COPYRIGHT

An Unbreakable Bond:
The Ultimate Mother & Daughter Relationship
ISBN-13: **978-1-7338592-0-2**

Copyright ©2019 by Tracey Hines

Published by
BALM2 Productions, Inc.
Brooklyn, NY

Printed in the United States of America.
This book or parts thereof may not be reproduced in any form, stored in a retrieval system, or transmitted in any form by any means – electronic, mechanical, photocopy, recording or otherwise- without prior written permission of the publisher, except as provided by the United States of America copyright law.

This book is available at special quantity discounts for bulk purchase for sales promotions, fund-raising and educational needs. For information please write fulleffectmail@aol.com.

Cover Design by Daiheem Kearse for Prophetic Imaging

DEDICATION

In Memory
of my immediate family that has departed but is very present in our hearts:

My Parents,
Warren Albert Pickens and Lillie Dell Phillips

My Sisters,
Frances Odell Phillips Goodwin and
Robin Renee Pickens McDuffie

My Nephews,
Woody Allen Goodwin and Jeffrey Larue Pickens, Jr.

To My Legacy
Kola Ivy Hines Roberts, Son-n-law Ryan Alexander Roberts, Sr. my grandson Ryan Alexander Roberts, II (aka Deuce) and all my grandchildren and my children's children for generations to come. I wrote this with all of you in mind. ***Keeping Our Legacy Alive!***

ACKNOWLEDGMENTS
Special thanks to

My siblings, Cheryl Paul, Cynthia Brewster, and Jeffrey Pickens for always caring for me, protecting me and always wanting to see me do well.

My awesome niece Montrice Brewster aka Pumpkin who loves me and thinks the world of me and believes me to be great. My nieces Cassidy Paul and Frances Lavon Goodwin Flemming who always enjoys talking with me and speaks well of me.

My dearest friends who has always supported me throughout years and genuinely want to see me succeed, Jasmine Degeneste, Susan Green, Lonzel McNeil, and Paulette Elliott.

Over the years these ladies have inspired me when they have occasionally received my counsel and words of encouragement. Shaniequa Ratliff, Darlene Crowder, Jennifer Dawson, Kira Kennedy, Chenoa Yokum, Alicia R. Kearse, Shantel Harden, Shamel Freeland, Elicia Khan, Nephetia Brown, Olivia Bryant, Sekoya Issacs, and Myechia Cartwright- Hooper, just to name a few.

Mother Mary Johnson, Mother Beverly McInnis and Bishop Archie McInnis Sr. for stepping in as Grandparents for Kola, accepting her as one of your grandchildren and showing her love and concern. Even babysitting from time to time. Much love for you all.

My Writing Made Easy Coach, Wanza Leftwich for your divine instruction and guidance that opened the writer side of me. Your ability to unlock and tap into the creative side of me was an ultimate blessing.

My First Lady Dr. Cynthia McInnis for always praying for me and Kola. Always being a mighty inspiration and awesome example. Teaching me to let time be my ally. This allowed me to dream again and begin again and move in the new vision. Grateful for you believing in me and writing the foreword. I am overwhelming thankful.

My Bishop Archie L. McInnis, for giving me the opportunity to go forth in my gift. All your prayers, spiritual counsel and sound doctrine. The awakening message preached December 31, 2017 in the Watch Night Service – he proclaimed 2018 Year of Breakthrough! I caught hold of that message and ran the course and will continue. He spoke in my life… "My latter shall be greater! There is more to come from this point forward." I am now seeing the manifestation of that declaration. I am forever grateful.

I am forever thankful and grateful for all the love and support you all have shown me. May heaven smile upon you all and God richly bless each one of you! This is my earnest prayer! Thank you from the depths of my heart.

FOREWORD

An Unbreakable Bond by Tracey Hines has left me in awe of the power of mother-daughter relationship and overall *storge'* love. Admittedly, at first glance, although I have a daughter, I found little or no interest in a story about a mother-daughter relationship. In my opinion, all relationships are different, but Tracey has found a way to tell her truth in a very colorful and insatiable way. I found myself engrossed with reading page after page; laughing out loud *with* her, crying real tears *with* her and *feeling* every season *with* her.

To say that Kola is an interestingly amazing young lady seems to be a very bland description. In so many ways, Kola is me and Kola is you. Her innocence is portrayed throughout the story in such magnificence that I almost believed it was my childhood being reenacted. While we shared a completely different environment and set of circumstances, the child-like, little-girl-in-me innocence was strangely the same! I thought those thoughts! I felt those feelings! I cried those tears. I loved that love and I cussed those cuss words privately, in my mind or under my breath.

Every mother will want to read this book. Every father would want to see himself through the innocent eyes of his son or daughter and every caregiver will benefit from a walk with Tracey and Kola through the delightfully entertaining, painful but powerful truth found in the footprints of An Unbreakable Bond.

Humbly submitted,
Dr. Cynthia McInnis
Author, Playwright, Filmmaker & Executive Administrator of Full Effect Churches Worldwide

An Unbreakable Bond

Table of Contents

An Unbreakable Bond	i
COPYRIGHT	ii
DEDICATION	iii
ACKNOWLEDGMENTS	v
FOREWORD	vii
New Life	3
The Stand	14
The Ants	24
Double "D's"	30
Lesson Learned	43
The Decision	49
Moment to Remember	62
Who is this Child?	79
Unexpected Events	93
A New Beginning	106
About the Author	111

Tracey Hines

An Unbreakable Bond

Chapter One

New Life
"A Seed with Purpose"

Cousin Eleanor Davis sat comfortably in her La-Z-Boy reclining chair. I was taken aback by how this once beautiful golden brown complexioned woman with beautiful hair, was now fully gray-haired and looked small, frail and thin sitting in her recliner. I must say with me being 6 months pregnant and having difficulty getting in and out of chairs, that recliner was looking so inviting. I was so happy when Cousin Eleanor offered for me to sit in it. I graciously accepted and immediately put my feet up. My momma shot me the eye as if to say, "How you going to let your elderly cousin who is old enough to be your grandma get up from her chair? You 25 years young." I turned a blind eye as if I didn't know she was giving me the eye. Oh, but I knew when my mom got me alone she was going to let me have it. I could almost hear the conversation.

It would go something like this: You young people get pregnant and you act like you can't do nothing. When I was pregnant with you, I had you in the belly, Jeffrey in one arm and Cynthia holding me by the hand, Cheryl, Robin and Frances were much older than you three. All you have is one and you act like you can't function. My mom was a boisterous southern woman, the matriarch of our family. She made it clear and she would say to all her children, "I don't care how grown you get, you will never be grown as me."

I snuggled up in that big recliner and I was certain to tell my husband, "I want this recliner." I was so comfortable; I knew I could sleep in this chair. Lord knows I have the hardest time getting good sleep between the bathroom trips and peeing every waking second, and Kevin waking me up, saying "I was watching your stomach while you slept. It looks like the baby be stretching all the way out in there. I'm just checking to see if you are in any pain." I swear I wanted to strangle him sometimes. All I said was, "If I didn't wake up, or I didn't move, and you see me still asleep, don't wake me up and ask if I am in pain."

An Unbreakable Bond

As comfortable as I was in Cousin Eleanor's recliner, the baby was kicking or punching me. It felt like the baby was hitting a punching bag inside and I was it. It felt like it was connecting some good right and left hooks. They would hurt me really bad, but I made it a point not to tell anyone, especially after the fear early in the pregnancy when the doctor put me on bed rest for two weeks. My sister Cheryl stayed one week with me and my sister-in-law Rochelle stayed a week with me. They each were wonderful to be around. They catered to me. They made sure I had whatever I needed, because Kevin worked night shifts and sometimes he did doubles, and he didn't want me alone at all. I literally was advised to only do the bed and the bathroom.

During that period of time the baby's brain was developing. The doctor said I was beginning to show spots of blood, which could be Placenta Previa, where the baby detaches itself from the umbilical cord. In other words the baby was beginning to abort itself. I was thanking God as I was relaxing in the recliner that the baby was way past that stage of being in danger. The baby was beginning to show signs of possibly being an 8 lb. baby. I was so very grateful. I had to talk to the baby while it was in my stomach. I was apologizing, asking the baby to forgive Mommy for smoking cigarettes, sipping on wine coolers, sitting up late hours playing cards for money and even going roller skating during the early stages of the pregnancy. I didn't have morning sickness or any other signs to show I was pregnant except no menstrual cycle. My pregnancy was great. I had functioned as if I wasn't pregnant, so I could understand the baby wanting to abort itself from me. The baby probably thought, *Wow! Let me check out, there is no love here.*

In walked my cousin Wesley Davis who was Cousin Eleanor and Bubba's son. He was our cousin, but he was more like an older brother. He'd had a rough start in life, but made a major turnaround, and did well for himself. He went on to marry a beautiful lady named Yvonne Singleton. She was a school teacher, classy and well put together. She stayed by Wesley's side through it all until his dying day. Whenever I saw Wes, I thought he was a handsomer version of Marvin Gaye, like the way he looked on the cover of his album *What's Going*

An Unbreakable Bond

On. Everybody thought Marvin Gaye was fine, but I thought my cousin had him beat.

He was about 6'2, nice build, was always dressed sharp and clean as a whistle, we would say. But what kept me in fascination with my cousin was he was tall and strong, bad to the bone, but just as humble and baby boyish, like when it came to his momma. She was little, petite and frail, but when she called out to him, "Wes, come over here," he'd turn and say, "Ma, you call me?" and she'd say, "Fix me a glass of water," and he'd go do it." I was so fascinated seeing how humble this big man was when it came to his momma.

It was watching them that made me know I wanted to have a son. I knew Kevin and I were having a son and my mind prepared me for that. I didn't even consider a girl's name. I knew I was going to have this fine son, tall, strong, independent, not a statistic and thought about how he would take care of me when I am old and gray. So being super-duper excited that I knew in my entire being I was having a son, I told my husband Kevin what I thought. He flat out told me not so. He said, "We are having a daughter. I told you the day we found out you were pregnant. I said then, 'I made a girl.' I even can tell you where and when we made it. It's a girl. Now we need to get a name for a girl." I said, "I never thought of a name for a girl because I always thought it was a boy. I believe it more now than ever."

As usual, the family started discussing what they thought I was having. Of course everyone goes by the usual, "Oh, she's round like this; it's a girl, or someone would say, "Oh no wait, she's not swollen, nor does she get morning sickness; that's definitely a boy." Kevin said, "Mother, I don't know about all those signs; I just know she's having a girl. She's carrying my Little "G." Well from that time up until a month before my due date, my husband had to work a double shift.

One particular day it was storming outside. The rain was heavy and the thunder was loud and the lightning was extremely bright in the room. Kevin called me, which was very surprising because he never believed in being on the phone when there was a storm. I could tell from his voice he was crying. When I asked him what happened, he said, "I felt the presence of my mom and she said we must name our daughter COLA." I said, "Oh no, poor girl they're going to tease her. They're going to spell it like soda." He said, "No, use "K." It means something. Keeping Our Lord Alive!

I was in tears. Just to think the week before, we were bumping heads because he was determined I should come up with a girl's name. So I told him, "It's a boy, I don't have to figure out a name; it's going to be Kevin Jr., but I will call him Ellis because I love that name." He said, "You better stop thinking it's a boy. A father knows. So what girl name did *you* have in mind? He, asked." I said, "When we consider a name, we need to make sure it won't hurt their chances when they are an adult. We don't need our child prejudged before even being met, based solely on their name. I think we should also think of what profession we can see them in and name them accordingly. If it's a girl, you can name her Alia Monet, that's the name of a singer on an album cover. Or Ayanna Leslie, Esq. Attorney-at-Law.

"You got to be out your mind Tracey!" He told me. "Of course you are going to say no; why bother to ask me?" I told him, "Because you need to know it's a girl and start thinking about it." So, I asked him, what do you have in mind. He said, "Let's use my mother's name, Sandra." I said, "No, Sandra is too old." He then said, "How about your mom's name then? Lillie Dell or LaDell." I said, "No." That's too close to your ex-girlfriend's name. You have to come up with something better."

To hear him give the name KOLA with a meaning warmed my heart. I started saying things like, "Hello, Dr. Kola," nobody can tell if it's a boy or girl by this name. Then I started pretending I was calling her. "Kola, come upstairs." "Hello, did anybody see Kola?" "Kevin, you need to buy Kola some more pampers." Oh yeah. This name Kola will work. Soon as I agreed to name her Kola, he made me write in my journal and sign it that I would name the baby Kola if it's a girl. Long story short, after 17 hours of labor, this 7 lb. 14 oz., 22-inch long, beautiful, one tone, non-scaling skinned, cocoa brown baby girl with straight, jet black hair arrived on the scene on April 2, 1992.

When they placed her on my chest, her hand glided across my face. We were instantly bonded. Our secret joke was that she slapped me for all that I put her through while she was in me. I even whispered to her, "This is the first and last time you get to raise your hand to me." It amazes me how I can remember that day as if it were yesterday. After delivering her in the hospital, I was left alone in my room, getting sleep that was much needed. I jolted and sat upright, heart beating fast and in a cold sweat; it just hit me that I had a daughter.

All my thoughts and mind preparations were to raise a son. I was 25 years old, married 4 years and now the mother of a daughter. Never thought about how to raise a girl child. I had a gorgeous niece Lavon who was my age, my beautiful niece Montrice who I adored and called Pumpkin and she was 4. I always bought her clothes and anything I wanted her to have. I didn't get to babysit her much, I was not about babysitting children during those days. My sister Cheryl, her other auntie, always had my niece with her. She was so attached to her, everywhere my sister Cynthia and her husband Julius took her too, Cheryl was sure to follow. My niece Montrice was the center of all our joy. Then there were my nephews Woodro, Rasheen, Jeffrey Jr. and Larue. So, all my thoughts were about the baby being a boy. I then began to panic, thinking, *I have to protect this child against the world.* I jumped out of the bed with the mind to go get this little girl who I wasn't prepared for but already filled with the idea that it would be us against the world. I knew I would protect her with every fiber of my being.

Soon as tried to get out of the bed, I fell to the floor like a rag doll. Because I'd had an Epidural my legs buckled, which was the side effect of having a needle in your spine, plus perhaps too much medicine. Nonetheless I struggled up from the floor and gathered as much strength as possible and went to see my baby in the nursery. While in the nursery I couldn't believe how fascinated the nurses were with her skin. Kola's skin wasn't scaly or peeling or blotchy. She has cocoa brown smooth skin. The nurse said, "We know you did the right things while carrying her. You must have taken all of your prenatal vitamins and of course the iron pills to get that smooth skin and to have that even skin tone."

It's amazing how this baby girl of mine who was growing inside of me endured all that I went through while I was carrying her. My emotional and physical rollercoaster. As I kept looking at her, I could only say, "Thank God He covered my baby in the womb."

As I watched her I thought, *Kola, this is a new life for you and it's a new life for me too. Please, little one, bear with me as we start this new life journey.*

Chapter Two

The Stand
"When age or position doesn't matter"

"I love you, you love me, we're ah happy family, with a great big hug and a kiss from me to you, won't you say you love me too!" She is a die-hard Barney fan. Cooing to the melody already. At 3 months she already knows what's going on. I was determined from the start that we would not be doing "goo goo or ga ga". We will speak English straight from the womb. Everything I did for her or with her I spoke it. My neighbors would have thought I had other people around, the way I was talking to this baby. I would say, "Kola, Mommy's going to give you a bath in your yellow tub. I will put your green skirt and blouse on. I'm going to warm your bottle. Let's make Daddy dinner. Let's make his favorite meal. Do you want to go outside and get some fresh air?" It was important that she understand language and if she heard me speaking to her directly, she would comprehend early on and have an attention span to be alert.

An Unbreakable Bond

On one particular day we went to my mom's house. I told Kola, "We are going to Grandma's house. She is going to watch you while Mommy goes to the hair salon. Mommy will be back." My appointment was a little longer than usual and I was unable to be at my mom's by the time my husband Kevin came to get us. When her dad tried to dress her, Kola cried and twisted and turned. She was only five months. Her dad said, "Let me call her mom. I know Tracey, didn't tell her I was picking her up; that is why she is fussing." So he called the hair salon. I spoke with him and he put the phone to her ear. I said, "Kola, Mommy's hair appointment took longer. Let Daddy dress you. He's going to bring you to come get me, and then we all will go home."

My mom got on the phone and said, "I can't believe what I am seeing. This little one stopped fussing, and put her arm in the sweater like she understood what you said." I knew then my baby girl was taking a stand. I told my mom I should have told her that her dad might be picking her up. I normally tell her everything that we are going to be doing. I knew if I would made it a point to talk to her early like she was a little person, it would help with her development. She was unable to speak back to me, but she could comprehend. My mother was fascinated that Kola comprehended like that and it was evident so early on. She said Kola was like, *I know you're here, Daddy, but Mommy didn't tell me you were coming.*

Oh, her Dad knows how to talk to her. He didn't feel bad about it. That's why he wanted to call me, because he knew if I didn't tell her something, Kola would become fussy. He knew that being a stay-at-home mom, I was developing a routine and building a mother-daughter relationship right away. It's amazing that some mothers only provide the care for their daughters as far as dressing them with matching outfits and doing girly things. Especially doing the hairdos. Most of the time that will be the focus. It's important early on to build a Mother –daughter relationship. When it comes to children, be it boy or girl, we nurture them physically when they are babies. We must also nurture them emotionally and guide and instruct them early. Study our children right out the womb. Some wait until they are walking and talking. I think that's too late. When your child is eight months and slapping your face, you must start right there because soon those little hands get bigger. Then they will embarrass you in the street. I discovered no matter what you do with your child, at some point that child will try you. That goes for every stage.

I vividly remember a particular time when Kola was two years old. She had a light pink snowsuit on. It was in the winter months and the ground was wet from the melted, dirty snow. Kola and I had just left the supermarket, heading home. As we were walking, she stopped and wanted me to pick her up, but I had two bags of groceries in my arms. She decided to fall out on the ground and roll over, throwing a temper tantrum. I couldn't believe this little girl just did this out in the street. Oh! My skin was boiling. This little girl was determined to embarrass me out in the street. So I put the bags down on the ground and bent down to pick her up, then I saw the look on her face that said, *I got her*. I stood straight up and took a stand. I thought, *Oh! you will not be thinking you can behave like this*. I moved to the side and leaned against a parked car and smoked my cigarette.

I told everybody who walked by, wanting to pick this cute two-year-old kid up, "That's my child. She's throwing a tantrum. She'll be okay." When they asked me about picking her up, I said, "Thanks, but no thanks. I have to take a stand now and show her you don't get what you want by throwing tantrums and that she don't run me. If I don't stop it now, I will be in more trouble later." People were saying, "I hear that." After that people started saying, "Aw cutie, you must listen to Mommy. You have to walk." She got up and did the same thing a few more times. By the fifth time she realized, *Mommy's not picking me up* and she walked all the way home, holding on to the bag like she was helping me carry it. She learned a valuable lesson because that was her first public display and her last. I took a stand. When we got home, I told her, "Mommy wanted to pick you up, but I couldn't. Now that my arms are empty, I can pick you up and hug you and kiss you." She understood that Mommy may want to say yes, but sometimes she will have to say no."

An Unbreakable Bond

I can recall about a year later at three years old, she took a stand for me. Kola and I were visiting my mom as we did often. My sister Robin, aka Beanie, was there making bread pudding. She knew I was coming and that was one of my favorites. Robin's bread pudding would have the house smelling delicious. She knew I loved it with a lot of raisins and she needed some extra raisins, so I told her I would run and get her some from the corner store. She was happy and advised me to leave Kola, so I could go and come back faster. When I left out the door, Momma told Robin, "I don't know why Tracey put that dress on. I don't think she should have worn that dress." Kola stood up and screamed, "No, Grandma, don't talk about my momma!" Well, my mother turned to Kola and said, "That's my daughter and I can say what I want. I am her mother." Well, Robin was so fascinated that my daughter did not take into account how big my mother was compared to her, nor who she was. All she knew with her little 26 lb. self, under 3 feet, nobody was going to dishonor her momma. Robin said, "You thought you needed a son to protect you, but that little Kola is going to protect you and Kevin. You two will not have to worry about nothing. That one kid right there will make up for five kids." God bless my sister Robin, she was speaking prophetically; Kola truly has been just that to her father and me.

Soon after this Kola and I had another moment of taking a stand. It was one of those rainy days when I wasn't going out of the house. Kola wanted me to play with her. My playtime with her was doing flashcards so she could practice learning her colors, numbers and alphabet. Learning Sesame Street characters. Learn and play. She will be going to daycare with a teacher in the classroom with other kids. Prior to day-care she was nurtured and taught by Ms. Frankie Baker. She was the absolute best home child-care provider in town. She prepared your child for the daycare setting. I loved how she and her family loved and cared for my daughter. Her daughter Billie Joe was a hard-working sister, but she loved on the kids when she got home, and they couldn't wait to spend time with her.

Well, because Kola always had someone to play with her there, she figured I would do the same at home. So she said, "Mommy, play with me." I said, "No." She said, "Mommy, play with me." I said, "No." She started looking like she would cry. I pointed my finger at her and said, "I don't have to play with you if I don't want to. What happens when you're in daycare if nobody wants to play with you? What are you going to do? You don't play. You have toys, you have a brain. If there is something you want to play, then you play. You don't cry. If nobody plays with you, then you go play by yourself." It hurt me to tell her that with her being so little, but all I could see was her as a teenager, begging somebody to play with her and then doing things to get people to like her. I had to show her I was mommy and I didn't have to play with her and neither did anyone else.

Next Kola attended Waverly Daycare with an awesome teacher named Ms. Tate. Kola was very dainty. I loved to dress her with skirts, ruffled socks and patent leather shoes. I came to pick her up on one particular day, and Ms. Tate said, "I need to speak with you for a moment, Ms. Hines. I immediately felt maybe Kola was really too little to be in daycare. All of the kids in her class were bigger. She was such a little child but strong and smart. She said, "We have a student who is very aggressive in the class and all the kids are afraid of him. The children tell us that he takes the toys from them and makes them cry. Some reported that he pushed them off the tricycle. We saw him push Kola off the tricycle. Just as we called for him to stop, and went to speak with him, Kola chased him down until he jumped off the tricycle, then she kept chasing him until he was tired and fell out on the mats. She bent down and slapped him. This dainty little ponytail girl with a skirt on, ruffled socks and patent leather shoes, jumped back on the tricycle and just rode off as if nothing happened. Well he met his match today, with your Kola. We stood there with our mouths wide open in disbelief. The other children were frozen as well, not believing that she was not afraid of this aggressive little boy.

"I must say, we were astonished. So we decided to bring the children inside and allowed them to play. Once all the little children saw that Kola stood up to this kid, they all wanted to play with her. Kola said, 'No, I don't want to play with anybody. I want to play by myself.' Do you know the children came crying and said, 'Kola doesn't want to play with me.'" The teacher continued, "I told those children, you find someone to play with or you do like she is doing and play by yourselves." I didn't know whether to be proud or embarrassed. I didn't know how to take what the teacher was saying to me. I wondered, what did I just start? Ms. Tate said, "What did you do to get this only child to be like that? Most only children are very needy and always looking for validation." I stood in disbelief. How did my little girl master that? She probably doesn't even know she learned a valuable lesson on how to stand up for herself and take charge and set the tone for what she wants. I realized then that she comprehends very well.

Chapter Three

The Ants
"Truth from one of the smallest creations"

"Kola, baby girl, I know you want to give every flower and leaf you see to Grandma, and I know she appreciates you always thinking of her, but I don't think we should bring them to Grandma today. She hasn't been feeling well lately. Today we should buy her a basket of fruit; she would like that. You can tell her all the names of the fruit you picked." "Mommy, is it Grandma's birthday?" Kola asked. "It's not Grandma's birthday. It's Just Because Day. Sometimes it's nice to do things just because you love." "Mommy, I want to buy two ring pops and you can have one just because. We have to get Pop-Pop ice cream just because. You have to buy Aunt Robin nacho cheese and cheese slices just because, and you have to make Aunt Cheryl a chocolate cake with white frosting and coconut sprinkles. Oh and Mommy, you have to buy Aunt Cynthia some sunglasses, and my Uncle Knucklehead

(Jeffrey), we have to buy him a watch just because. Mommy, everybody has to get a just because gift."

"Kola we are only getting a just because gift for Grandma today. Everyone else we will pick a day to give each of them a just because gift." "Mommy, why Grandma be in the bed a lot? Sometimes she be out in the kitchen, but when Ms. Emma Medina or Poochie (Myechia Cartwright) bring me home; Grandma stays in the room? She doesn't talk with Ms. Emma or Poochie anymore." "Kola, Grandma don't feel well some days, but they understand; they love Grandma. "Aunt Robin tells me to stay in the room with her. Grandma calls me sometimes, but I don't always hear her, Pop-Pop will call me; and she let me lay down with her. Then sometimes we go there and she's playing her music and looking out the window. I like when Grandma is like that. Mommy, when Grandma is feeling good, she makes the beef with the rope and the little potatoes and she lets me help her with the string beans. Can we do that?" "Yes, we can. Baby girl, we have to go get the bus while the sun is up."

As we were leaving, I could not believe how beautiful it was outside. Yet, I could barely enjoy any day. My heart's joy was leaving me. I had to carry the weight of knowing that my Momma was dying of cancer, Robin was sick and Momma was worried about Robin. Mommy made me her health proxy and told the family not to tell other family and friends that she had cancer. She also request that we do not to allow any doctors to give her chemotherapy or experimental operations. "Just let me go home to my Maker," Momma told all of us. "All of my kids are grown," Momma would say to us. "I asked the Lord to keep me here until my kids are grown. My God did just what I asked of Him. I know I am a child of God. My baby is 30 years old. I have seen all my kids get married and my grandbabies. You all have to take this time to get things together."

The pain of this knowledge made me sick literally. I had stomach ulcers. I couldn't hold my bowels. One day coming to visit my mom, Kola and I walked through the park and my bowels gave way. Kola laughed, she didn't understand it was my nerves. She was being a child. She said, "Oh, Mommy, you boom-boom on yourself. I don't do that anymore, now you do." Every day, I carried the weight of how I was supposed to tell my five year old her Grandma who she loved dearly, was dying. As we stood at the bus stop on our way home, Kola screamed, "Mommy, Mommy, look at all the ants?" "Yes, I see them. I am going to step on them and kill them." So I raised my foot and squashed all of them. Kola said, "Mommy, you killed them. Oh look, Mommy, one got away. Kill it!" I said, "No. I'm not going to kill it." Kola said, "Mommy, why didn't you kill it?" "I didn't kill it because it didn't follow the crowd." I paused, knowing it was time to tell her.

"Kola, Mommy's got something to tell you. We are going to be staying at Grandma and Pop-Pop's house during the week, Monday through Friday, then on Saturdays and Sundays we will stay at our house." "Yay! Mommy, I love when we stay with Grandma and Pop-Pop. You know Aunt Robin has Cousin Rasheen buy me Honey Buns." "That's nice."

Let me tell you why we have to stay there? We all have to help take care of Grandma. On the weekdays during the daytime Pop-Pop and Aunt Robin take care of Grandma, and Aunt Cheryl comes and helps, but she has to take care of her baby girl Cassidy. She helps take care of Grandma's banking business. Aunt Cynthia has two jobs during the week, so she and Uncle Jeffrey will help on the weekend. During the week at night when I get off work, I'll take care of Grandma.

I will feed and bathe her at night. You can help me. That will be nice. I will even let you help pick out Grandma's nightgown, test the water and make sure it's warm enough. We can put the lotion and powder on Grandma to make her smell nice. Then you can put the straw in the cup, so she can have her soup. It's going to be fun. We can make Grandma laugh and I will read to her." "Yay! Mommy, I want to help take care of Grandma." "Great! Oh, Baby girl, you're going to sleep in the room with Aunt Robin. I will sleep in the chair in Grandma and Pop-pop's room, just in case Grandma needs me in the middle of the night. Pop-pop need to rest because when I take you to daycare and go to work, Pop-pop and Aunt Robin have to take care of Grandma. Baby girl, you notice Grandma needs help, right? Grandma is very, very sick and we have to do whatever part we can to help her feel better. "Mommy, I want to do my part." "Good, I want to do my part too." "Mommy, I am going to do this for you too." "Do what?" "Take care of you just like you take care of Grandma. Just like I put the Band-Aid on your knee when you had your boo boo and I brought you water. I can help take care of Grandma." "Baby girl, you make me very happy! I know Grandma will be very happy to see you help her."

Chapter Four

Double "D's"
"Divorce and Deaths – One and the Same"

"Momma, you think you up to sitting in the kitchen for a little while? Robin's going to cook, maybe you can pop the beans. I'll go put on your record, "The Golden Gospel Jubilee." "Sure, I can," Momma said. Daddy said, "Your momma not strong enough to go out there. Just put the music on and turn it up for your momma to hear it back here." "Tracey, come here," Robin called. "Yeah?" I answered. Robin said, "You have to talk to Mommy and tell her she has to let us tell people. Her sister's calling, Emma and Arthur, Cora and Charlene want to know what's going on. They love Momma just as much as we do. Arthur is going to be a mess. You know he sees her as his momma. You know his own momma used to call our momma. She knew Arthur saw himself as our family and Momma and Daddy made him their son; he saw himself as our brother." Now Robin was always the rough one and didn't really care for anyone's feelings. To hear her say that, I knew it was time. Cheryl, Cynthia and Jeff already said to do it. At that point it was unanimous. I had to tell them. As Robin and I were talking, a certain song was playing "Blessed Assurance" and Momma was whispering the lyrics. "I love this song, play it again."

"Momma," Robin said, "Aunt Nettie, Emma, Arthur, Cora, Charlene and others have been stopping by and calling because they haven't heard from you. Ms. Sadie and Ms. Preston asked about you. You know, Pouncy always asks about you. Momma, people love you. We don't want nobody to think we're doing something to you. Well, they know we're not doing anything to you, but they know something is wrong. Cousin Wes came by here not long ago asking for you. Told him you were sleep and under the weather. Momma, you got to let us tell them." Momma said, "I don't want them crying and worrying. Somebody's going to have to watch Arthur, you know. I don't want him going off the deep end. You know Emma and Joe are worried. Cora is going to be crying. She's real sensitive. Charlene's going to be scared. Those my children too, you know. I don't want nobody crying and fussing over me. Be normal. That Poochie isn't going to take it well. Cora is going to have to be strong for her. So how you want us to do this? Don't call nobody. Names I said are the ones you tell and tell them what I told you." "Ok, Momma, we will."

As I recall that day we were all together. I think Cheryl told them and just as Momma said they would handle it, they did just that. The unity of the family in 157 N. Elliott Walk was amazing. Being raised in Fort Greene projects on the side we called The Island, each 6 story building was one family. The floor you lived on, you all were one family. Then, all the families in the building looked after each other. Oh, but according to the other sides of the projects, we looked after each other. If we traveled outside of the projects, if you saw anybody from your project you just knew you were okay. That was our way of showing community unity. A family! We could fight each other, talk about each other, but let some outsider come in and have some troubles with somebody in our neighborhood that we could have just had a fight with. Well they would team up and beat the lights out of someone.

Telling our extended family what was happening even though we told them towards the end, we had to respect her wishes. Sometimes I wonder if we really told them, or if I wanted so bad to tell them that I couldn't think that we didn't. Now I have to tell Kevin. We'd been separated for three years, being on again and off again to the point we just decided to be off. He would get Kola every other weekend. This man is 6'2" fine as wine, and I have to say what I look for in a man today, he was all that and then some back then, but I was too young to recognize it. Such is life; you live and you learn.

"Kev, we need to get together. I need to talk to you about what's been going on." He said, "Ok, tell me when and where." "Maybe we can meet at Kola's daycare and take her to the park on Washington Avenue on Dekalb side." He said, "Ok." It was very comforting to know that although he and I didn't work as a couple, we worked well as parents and have genuine concern for each other. He always knew when something was bothering me. He knew when I was coming down with a cold and when I was on my cycle. He has always been in tune with me. I often wonder why I walked away from him when all he wanted was his family. As he said, "If you don't want me, I am not going to force you. I am certainly not waiting for you to figure it out. I want a family. I am not a street man or a user. I respect woman and I want a wife not a girlfriend. Let's divorce so I can find a wife."

It's amazing that what you want, you tend to give away because you think you can so easily get it again. Sad truth is when you discover that all the time you were going through, all you saw was what you didn't like over what you did. Then you see all that you ever wanted you already had. It's a shame that it takes a lot of heartache and unnecessary troubles that you brought upon yourself because you thought you were all that and a bag of chips and find out your far from being all that. So there we were, sitting on the bench on a nice early spring day right before Kola's fifth birthday and Cassidy, my niece's first birthday. Kola's birthday is April second and Cassidy's is on the eleventh, Pop-Pop's on the fifteenth and Lavon's is on the twentieth. So much to celebrate in April. "Kevin, I'm just going to come out and tell you, my Mother is dying." Immediately my heart began to beat fast and I started gasping for air. I kept saying to him, "I can't breathe." He grabbed my face with both hands and said, "You can breathe, you are breathing. Relax. Count with me. One, two, three, four, five… if you count, your mind can't think on what you just said." That was anxiety. He said, "I knew something was wrong. I could see you lost a couple of pounds and Kola said she sleeps in the room with her Aunt Robin and you sleep in the chair in your parents' room." I explained the whole ordeal.

Last year, April 11, 1996, my sister Cheryl was having my beautiful niece in the hospital on one floor, while my sister Robin was in the same hospital on another floor in a coma with tubes everywhere and down to 90 lbs. and the doctors couldn't tell us what was wrong. I remember standing close to Mommy with such joy and happiness over the birth of her granddaughter. She was looking at her with a smile full of love. Then we went to the next floor and it hurt to see her heart ache for her daughter who had aged right before her eyes with all the tubes and monitors hooked up to her. She walked into the room, put her hand on her head and said, "Robin, what's wrong with you? How did this happen to you?" The nurse told us she could hear us, so I told her Cheryl had had a beautiful little girl. "You have to see her, she is so precious." I let her listen to Yolanda Adams sing "The Battle is the Lord's" on my Walkman. I asked the nurse if I could leave the Walkman with her and if she would check in on her from time to time and turn it over for her. She said she would.

Three days after Cheryl was released to go home with the baby, Robin was released. Before Robin came home, Momma was in Robin's room sitting on that stool Daddy made just for Momma at just the right height so she could rest her elbows on the window sill edge. He even placed a piece of plush carpeting on it to cushion her elbows. As I watched her she didn't even realize I was in the room. I said, "Momma, are you alright? When she turned and looked at me to speak, I was standing at the doorway entrance to the room and she was speaking past me. She said, "I don't understand what has just happened to my child. How she is 90 lbs. and I am 225 lbs.? She's sick and aging, looking so old. My children are to bury me, not the other way around. What is this thing?" I responded, "They are running all kinds of tests on her. I'm sure they will let us know. She had pneumonia and that's why she was in the coma. Why she's losing the weight, I don't understand. Robin eats good and doesn't eat a lot of outside food. I am worried about Rasheen. He lost his dad two years ago. He can't take seeing his mother sick." Although I was talking to my momma, it didn't feel like I was talking to her. It felt like something just happened that I couldn't explain, but I knew I was there for a reason and it was something I was never to forget.

"Kevin, I need you to help me. If you can keep Kola doing fun things, I'd appreciate it. She knows something is going on, but she doesn't know what. I didn't tell her Momma is dying. I said the words to you, but I haven't been saying those exact words. I told my job the doctors said she only has a few months. They called me at the job and even came to the house. Dr. Shaikh loves Mommy. He has been the family doctor for years. He feels like family. So many times Daddy or Robin and Cynthia would call me and say Mommy's asking for you. She wants you".

My bosses were Mr. Friedman and Ms. Bellouny. They would send me home in a company car just so I could be there. Ms. Bellouny said to me something I will never forget, she said, "I feel for you and I know it's painful, but at least you get to say goodbye your way. My sons and I were on our way to visit my mom just like we did every Saturday, spoke to her and said we were on our way. Get there, open the door and she was dead in her chair. She had a heart attack while we were on our way. My sons will never forget that. I never got to say goodbye. So much I could've said and didn't. So much I want to say and can't. Cherish these moments."

"Kev, sooo" (heavily sighing and chain smoking. Up to a pack and a half a day.) I can hear my boss, Mr. Friedman saying, "I would think you'd stop, knowing your mom has cancer." "He's right, and I feel ashamed and disgusted every time. Kev, if you can make sure to get Kola and help her enjoys herself as much as she can, but I need to be able to hold my baby girl as much as I can. She keeps me focused so I don't break down. She's too little and it will scare her. So that's why I let her help me bathe Momma. Kev, to see my mom go from 225 lbs. to 90 is devastating. But we talk to Momma like she healthy and strong. She doesn't feel ashamed and we don't have to be squeamish. I cry on my train ride to work. Just let the tears fall. This mother who has given life to six children who are all grown, and married with children, now her life is fading. Every day we watch her weaken and she is losing time. So much she will not see, hear, feel or do. There's absolutely nothing any of her children can do. I look in my siblings' eyes and we all have that same look. We all react differently, but we all feel the power of the inevitable. We all still look like children. Life and death go hand in hand.

By the way, I was putting all my papers together and I looked at the divorce decree. Do you know the date was the same date my mother was diagnosed with colon cancer? Thought that was ironic. Two death sentences. I'm not starting, and you know I'm not mad, I just was looking at that. In my head I was saying to myself what does this mean? Awww! Look at our baby on the big kid swing, little as she is. Kola! Kola!" "Come here, mama!" "Slow down, slow down didn't you see that boy riding by on his bike? Even though your Dad and I are here, you must always play and run as if we aren't here. Always protect yourself. Know what's going on around you."

"Tray...don't tell her that…we're her parents. We're here. She doesn't have to be like that, let her play free." "Kev. Of course we're watching her always, but she must consider where she is. You know I can be absentminded and I figure I'll catch her early from becoming absentminded. Let me get home. You can bring her to me whenever you want. Please make sure she's with me for the weekend. She can be with her cousin Montrice. She and her Aunt Robin also have their routine. Robin is now 225 lbs. and be cooking all the favorites you love. She looks so good. Would you believe, my sister Robin gave her life to the Lord? She told me to accept Jesus as my Savior. She said the whole family should give their life to the Lord. I told her we all accepted Jesus; I go to church on all the holidays. I make sure of that and I play my music, Kev, you know that.

An Unbreakable Bond

Every Sunday I blast my gospel music singing. But she said going to church and playing music isn't enough. You have to change your life. She said, "Some people be in church all the time and have four faces and are a bunch of phonies. She said we must take God seriously. You got to see Him in everything, Tracey'. I told Robin, when I am 55 I will give my life to the Lord. Right now, I am 30 yrs old and I am not trying to be nobody's Holy Roller."

Kev said, "I thought you gave your life to the Lord with me, when we used to go to Gospel Temple on Quincy Street. You remember Elder Wren and Mother Perkins? We used to go all the time. Tray, come on, remember Danita and Vincent? My brother Larry's sister. Dag, Tray, you don't remember how Larry's wife Kim, use to shout and her feet would move so fast? You used to ask her how she does that." "Wait…I remember going because you wanted too. I also remember you and I singing "We're going to make it," by Rev. Timothy Wright and Myrna Summers and look what happened to us. Nope, not I. Here I am, Divorced at 30 and my

Momma running out of time and dying and I am supposed to be in church a Holy Roller? Nope…not I."

Chapter Five

Lesson Learned
"Life in Death"

April 26, 1997 the day my life changed forever. My momma closed her eyes and left this world. My dad and all her children and their spouses were there except for Frances. She was on her way from down south. I can still see it clear as day. Montrice and Kola lay with their Grandma a little bit. I can recall Aunt Nettie saying, "She's leaving us, her breathes are, far and few." That early morning I lay with her and said, "Mom you can go. It's Okay. I'd rather you go than to stay and suffer for me. Go be with the Lord. We are going to be Okay." We all were in the house. "Daddy," Aunt Nettie said, "that's it. She's no longer breathing." Just like that, she drifted off and Momma was gone. I just stood there almost frozen, my mind couldn't comprehend what I was supposed to do next. Everyone started crying and tears rolled down my face. My siblings were all telling me, "Little sis, you did good taking care of mommy" I said,

"We all did our part." We all did what we could, considering our families and jobs. "You kids took care of my sister," Aunt Nettie said. Robin said, "Momma didn't want us to tell anyone and we had to do what she said." After that I couldn't hear anyone. I kept saying "I can't breathe." I just kept gulping big breaths. Kevin held me and had Kola in his arms and she was crying, he was crying and I just wanted to breathe. Kevin kept saying, "No matter who comes or who goes, I will always be here for you." *I can't breathe.* He said, "Count…" *I can't breathe.* "I need you to take Kola. I can't let her see them take her in a body bag. That cannot be in her memory." He said, "I worked in Woodhull Hospital as a darkroom technician and I saw a lot of bodies. When they come I'm going to be in there with them."

When they came to get her and when they took her body out of the room, the wailing that came from Apartment 4A was like no other. Time stood still, and the gateway that brought us into the world was closed. It was as if we all simultaneously felt disconnected. The link that kept the chain together broke off and all the other links just scattered not knowing where to connect.

The links were all only connected to the one link but not to each other and just like that everyone was lost. I wanted to scream, but I just stood there in Kevin's arms with Kola hugging me and her father. In her five-year-old little voice, "Mommy. You going to be ok, Mommy. I love you, Mommy. I'm with you, Mommy. Right, Daddy? I can take care of you, Mommy, like you took care of Grandma." "Oh! Baby girl, I love you too. I need you to go with Daddy, and I will get you on Monday." Kevin said, "You shouldn't be alone." "No, that's just what I need. I need to breathe. I need to get to my place. I'll be back here tomorrow; there is much to do."

As soon as I entered my place I screamed, crying uncontrollably and my dear neighbor Susan Green came upstairs and hugged me, expressing her condolences. She said she'd be right back, she was going to get the landlady Ms. Hilary. She came up and prayed. All I kept saying was *I can't breathe.* My phone was ringing off the hook. I told Susan to let the answering machine get it. It rang again, and it was my dear friend Jasmine DeGeneste. She said, "I been calling you for days. How's Mom?" I said, "She's gone. Mom died. I can't breathe.

I'm going to be sick." She said, "I am on my way." This friend has been true blue and there for just about every major event in my life. Always there. I was pregnant with Kola and I would have a craving for her hamburgers and grape Kool-Aid. I would call her at 1:00 a.m. for that burger when she had to be at work by 8:00 a.m. Kevin would get out the bed and drive me over. Her fiancé Greg and my husband would be stretched out head back dozing on and off, trying to sip on beer. I was in heaven. She was cooking and talking like its 1:00 in the afternoon. Not one ounce bothered by the time or that I woke her out of her sleep and she had a four year old to attend to. She said, "That's my godchild in there. Whatever the baby needs and wants I am there. By the way," she said, "What you want for your baby shower?" "I want a rocking chair; I saw it in Consumers." She said, "No problem, you got it. I will order it." "Jazz, it costs about $180." "Tray, did I ask you how much it costs?" "You know I don't roll like that. It's nothing I wouldn't do for my girls. You, Nancy and Mickey. I would give the shirt off my back." Until this day, those words are still true. She lives by them. A friend like no other. Worthy of great blessings.

The bell was ringing frantically and Susan let Jazz in and she had her little New Testament Bible with her. She said, "Breathe. I am going to read the Psalms." She started with Psalm 121 and kept reading it and Psalm 23. It was the only way I could fall asleep after she left. Pillow drenched with tears, all I could keep repeating was "Psalm 121:1, I will lift up mine eyes unto the hills, from whence cometh my help; 121:2 My help cometh from the LORD, which made heaven and earth." Asking God, "What am I supposed to do now? Momma is gone, and I am all alone. I saw Momma every day. I called every day. I knew this day had to come; I just don't know what to do now that it's here. Help me, God. I can't breathe. How am I supposed to do this and take care of Kola? She needed more time with her grandma. Why did this happen so fast? Six months ago she was diagnosed and now she's gone. What did I do wrong that she couldn't stay longer? What was I supposed to do as a daughter, as her last child? "I tried to make life easy for her as a child and not give her trouble. Why did she trade places with Robin? She wasn't supposed to go yet. We still needed her. Cassidy doesn't know who she is. How do we tell her? Oh! God this isn't fair. Not *this* parent. My parent wasn't supposed to die. Help me! *I can't breathe."*

The phone was ringing at 11 a.m. the day after. Kola was on the phone, "Mommy, Daddy made me a big breakfast. I told him to fix you a plate. I want to bring it to you. I can feed it to you too! Like the way you used to feed Grandma. Mommy, I love you, you love me, we're ah happy family, with a great big hug and a kiss from me to you. Won't you say you love me too?" I knew with tears coming down my cheeks that it was true: You can find life in death if you listen. Although Momma was gone, my heart ached for her, and tears were running down my face, but a smile was on my face for the joy of life I heard from Kola singing. The meaning of her name was becoming more evident. Amazing!

Chapter Six

The Decision
"Wrong Move and Right Outcome"

"Please, can you pick me up a lemon meringue pie from Blimpies Restaurant?" Robin asked. "Ok, no problem. Would you like a sandwich too?" I asked. She said, "No. Please also bring my Helen Baylor cassette." "Beanie, I was coming straight to you from the job. I wasn't going by Daddy's house. I guess I could go there and then come back to see you and go home from there." When I arrived at the hospital it caught me off guard. The nurse was assisting Beanie, fixing her pillows. I caught a real look at my sister; she was weaker and thinner than I realized. She was so happy I was there. I told her, "Of course you knew I was coming." She said, "Yeah, I knew you were coming. That's why I made you proxy, just like mommy made you proxy. You the youngest and you can get here quicker.

"It's ok, Robin, you my Yah-Hin." Robin said, "That's right, I took you with me everywhere." "Robin, you know in a couple of weeks Mommy will have been gone from us a year. Sometimes I feel like God was wrong. She could have still had some more years. She was talking about visiting her sister down south a little more. Having more gatherings with her dear friend Ms. Sadie. I recall her and daddy was trying to play matchmaker with Ms. Sadie and Mr. Hooks. I feel momma was gone to soon"

Robin said, "No one knows the day or the hour. When it's your time to go, nobody can do anything about it." I know that, I just sometimes feel angry with the world. I don't care about nobody but my immediate family. I feel like I'm becoming somebody who got a death wish. "Tracey, I don't want you talking and thinking like that Robin said. I look at her face there was a look of concern. You know I fought a cab driver in front of the cops. Literally punched the man in the face, he fell to his knees and the officer put my hands behind my back. Thank goodness I was taking Montrice to school. Montrice was crying and told the cop, 'The cab driver hit my aunt on her butt with his umbrella and threw it out the window. My aunt pulled him out the car, then you came.' The officer said, 'I could arrest you because I saw you hit him.'

"Robin, I feel so numb. I feel like it really doesn't matter what happens to me. If I didn't have Kola I sometimes think I would lose it altogether. Robin was just sitting there listening and shaking her head, no, no. She is in disbelief. I can tell she was getting flashbacks to how she used to be.

So I continued to tell her "You know I was in the corner store by my house with Kola. This lady was smoking a cigarette by the ice cream freezer in front of the counter. Kola was digging in the freezer getting her ice cream. The lady's cigarette ashes fell in Kola's hair. I went crazy. I could feel my eyes popping out my head. I charged this woman like a bull does when it sees red. I grabbed the lady, practically lifted her up off her feet. I threw her up against the rack of potato chips with my left hand, cocked back with my right arm about to swing on her and she threw her hands up. 'Miss, I am sorry. Miss, I am sorry.' I was mid-way into throwing her to the ground, when I heard my Kola's high pitched squeaky voice piercing through my crazy state screaming, 'Nooo! Mommy, nooo! You put ashes in my hair all the time!'

Robin said Thank God for my little niece. I told you she going to take care of you and Kevin. Tracey this could have gone very wrong. All, I know is "The adrenaline and rage that I was feeling immediately depleted and I went into a state of sheer embarrassment. I instantly wanted to hide my face from pure shame. I apologized to this lady profusely doing the bow of humility. Dusting her off to fix her clothes, and straighten her up. I offered to buy her something. I told her to get whatever she wanted. Then this little daughter of mine apologized to the lady, saying, 'My mommy didn't mean to hurt you.' The lady said, 'Oh, you so precious and such a pretty little girl. Don't you worry, your mommy did right, trying to protect you. I would have done what she did if I was her.' Talk about a double blow of humiliation and embarrassment, I wanted to crawl under the nearest rock. The man behind the counter was trying to give Kola candy, but she said, 'No, thank you.' He said, 'Get what you want.' She got herself two ice cream sandwiches. She got them for me.

Even though I was the one in error, she thought of me. I just grabbed her hand and all I could think was how stupid I was and how tragic things could have been. I could hear one of my Mommy's famous sayings in my head: God takes care of fools and babies. Clearly Kola is the baby and I sure enough was acting like a fool."

Robin was just sitting there on the bed shaking her head. I can almost see how her hearing this from me troubled her. She kept repeating, "Tracey, Tracey you can't be like that. Come on, Tracey, you know better than that. I'm telling you, listen to me, you know I had a lot of rage. I gave Jesus my heart. I gave Him all of me. I am happy, and I don't have rage anymore. I don't cuss. I take care of all my business. Everything is in order. I even be nice to my home attendant when she doesn't take care of me right. Tracey, you were always a sweet girl. Did well in school. You were a good girl."

"Robin, I'm fine. Just letting off a little steam. You tell me who stays good always? I guess it's my turn to mess up." Robin said, "Now you can't be thinking like that, Tracey. You got to think of Kola, because she is watching you. I think you really need to give your life to

Jesus. I watch Billy Graham and Charles Stanley. It doesn't take a lot. Everybody thinks it takes a lot to give themselves to Jesus. You just got to confess that Jesus died for you and rose for you. You just got to say it with your mouth and believe it in your heart, that's it. Then you live your life the way God wants you to. You do that, then you know you are a child of God. Tracey, you know one thing we all can say? Momma knew she was a child of God."

We laughed so hard because when momma said she was a child of God, she said it with such surety, and she didn't need no preacher or church to tell her that she belonged to God. She was baptized, and she knew Jesus saved her. She made you wonder if anybody else was or could be saved. Her faith was so strong. She would say, 'Please, I don't worry about nobody doing me no harm. God takes care of me.' You know I was paying attention to you and Mommy. How you gained all that weight. I just was looking at your chart and your weight is back down to 90 lbs." She said, "I know. Now I am the weight Mommy was when she passed away. Tracey, don't worry. I can get it back up like before."

An Unbreakable Bond

April 13, 1998, the hospital called me at 8 p.m. and said my sister Robin passed away. We went to go claim her body in the hospital morgue. When we arrived, and they escorted us to claim her. I was in shock! The peace that was on her face was incredible. There was no pained look or hurt look. She was actually smiling. She was almost glowing. Her skin looked like a baby's bottom. Never will I forget how she looked. That was incredible to me. My sister's life wasn't a bed of roses, but she was true about everything. She never sugar coated anything. She went through a period in her life where she would tell anybody off at the drop of a hat. Didn't matter what your position was in life.

I never will forget my wedding. I never showed up to the church to get married. I called it off. Kevin came to the house with the whole church and the reverend to marry me. That's a book of its own. So Robin told the reverend, "Come on and eat some of this ham and potato salad I made. Make sure you take a drink. We have a bar full of liquor; I am sure we have the brand you and your Deacons like to drink." Momma fussed with her a little. She said, "Robin, you don't talk to the reverend like that. Even if it's true, you still have to show respect." My sister Robin would say whatever came to her mouth. "What you see is what you get." She didn't have a problem with fighting anybody when it came to her family and friends. She would fight anyone, including men. Would knock a man out in a minute. Coming up she was very athletic and played a good game of basketball, handball and rode a mean bike. Beanie and my Cynthia would ride those bikes with no hands. Momma would look out the window and see Cynthia riding with no hands on the bars, sitting upright and she would get to fussing. I don't know why Beanie and Cynthia insisted on riding those bikes with no hands. It's amazing how death brings on a flood of random memories.

So here we go again. Geesh! God, you're really coming after me. Now I have to tell Kola her Aunt Robin died. I was just home from work for a week because my baby girl turned six years old on April 2nd, had a hernia operation on April 6th and then Beanie dies on April 13th. What is going on? I can't catch a break. How come all this is happening? I'm just becoming numb to life.

An Unbreakable Bond

Thank goodness for this little girl. If I didn't have to take care of her, I'm aware I would have just withered away. Robin and Momma were my world. Robin filled Momma's void because she was the closest to being mothering. I would put my siblings in categories. Robin (Beanie) was the protector and nurturer. If there was any trouble, you would go to Robin. If you wanted something to eat, Beanie would whip something up.

Cheryl was the instructor and keeper. She made sure we were together physically, and the house was kept clean. (Momma's right hand) and she made sure she was a good example, respectable, carried herself well, disciplined us to make sure we did right. Always wanted the best for us and gave us the best. Cynthia was only three years older than me. She was a walking adding machine. She was the bargainer. My brother Jeffrey, he was the determined one. Whatever he did, he had to master it. He and my dad worked hand in hand. My dad had a skill for working with wood designs and carpentry. Anything electrical. Jeff fixed every clock, watch, washing machine and refrigerator. Jeff also had a green thumb. I used to love to see him and my mom have their time. She would get that big bag of Miracle Grow fertilizer and they would sit there and repot the plants. Cutting and trimming, watering, talking to them, before you knew it, they would be growing. Me, I was the neutralizer. No matter what went on, I never took sides. I understood everybody's point of view with the truth. I would tell someone the truth even if they got mad. Still got that trait. If you don't want the truth, don't ask me.

So now I'm here still pondering how I'm going to tell Kola, honey bun to her Aunt Robin, that she died. Since I didn't really get to celebrate Kola on her 6th birthday because I had my mind on her surgery, I decided to focus on her and tell her easily and nonchalantly. My heart ached horribly when I was told my baby needed an operation. Her dad and I were together to hear the doctor explain the importance of the surgery and that it would not affect her having children. However, if we waited, no telling what problems could form. So we decided to let them operate. We took her to McDonald's, her favorite, to get the Happy Meal. She liked to collect the buckets and toys. We were sitting, and I was watching her, and the tears were about to fall and her father started crying uncontrollably saying, "Little Gee, you going to be Ok. You Daddy's big girl. Daddy don't want you to be scared." She got up and hugged her daddy saying, "Don't cry, Daddy. It's going to be Ok." He was crying on his little daughter's shoulder. I was watching them as I held my tears back. Couldn't have us both crying. But watching her comfort her daddy saying, "Daddy, my doctor has been a good doctor since I was born. She promised, so I believe her. I'm not scared, and I don't want you to be scared. Do you need to stay with me and Mommy?" He got himself together, and said, "No, Daddy has to work the night shift; I just came to make sure you were ok." "I'm ok, Daddy, Mommy takes care of me good."

I was happy he was there. Sad because I couldn't be vulnerable. Proud of how she was a little trooper. So I took her to Toys R Us and I just wanted to get her whatever she wanted. When we got there we saw a little blue-eyed, blonde-haired girl, same age as Kola, running around playing with everything, screaming, "Mommy, I want this and that." The mom said, "Ok, Susie, what color do you want? She never even looked at the price. I knew I had put $400 aside to splurge on her for a few outfits. I decided later, my child can get what she wants. I grabbed the cart. My daughter was thoughtful, "Mommy, can we afford to get this or that?" I said, "Baby girl, don't ask me if we can afford it. If you want it, put it in the cart. If it's a ticket item, grab it and bring it to me." She said, "Oh, Mommy, thank you." She took off and ran up and down the aisles. She would show me something and I would say, "Put it in the cart."

By the time she was finished, she had about 45 items and 10 tickets. So as we proceeded to the cashier, I told her, "Out of all these toys we are going to buy 6 of them. Make sure you pick the ones you want the most." She pulled out Play-Doh, a coloring book, a Slinky, a Barbie doll, a Curious George book, and a Little Mermaid video. It totaled up to under $100. I said, "Baby girl, you are such a great a little girl, Mommy's going to get six more toys and some clothes and sneakers. "Mommy," she hugged me so tight. "Thank you, Mommy. Thank you, Mommy. Can I get the Barbie sneakers with lights?" The cashier was smiling ear-to-ear with a twinkle in her eye like she wanted to cry. She

An Unbreakable Bond

said, "That is so nice! She is such a cute little girl and so grateful. Here." She gave her a miniature gumball machine. Kola looked at me as if to ask if it was ok to accept. I said, "It's okay, you can take it." She smiled at the lady. "Thank you!" The lady said, "Most kids would have just taken it. Even though she saw us talking, she waited for you to say ok. Oh, I like that," she said.

As we walked out of Toys R us, I realized because Kola had to touch all the toys she wanted, and pushed them in the cart, she felt they were hers already. When I told her to get what she really wanted, she dug down in the cart to find her items, bypassed all the expensive items and big items. I was fascinated. I told her always know what you want. If anybody ever asks you what you want, you make sure to tell them. Don't you worry about the price. "Mommy." "Yes, Kola?" "That nice lady has to put all those toys away that were in the cart." "Oh, you made that lady happy. She was ok with doing it this time. She had other workers helping her."

Chapter Seven

Moment to Remember
"Reflections"

"Momma, can we go to the $1.00 supply store? I want to spend my allowance on school supplies. I need construction paper, a box of pencils, erasers and pens. I don't like to lend the kids my supplies because they never return them or they lose my cap on the pen, break the pencils or erasers, so I'd rather sell it to them." "What? You do what, Kola?" "I sell them my supplies. Somebody always needs something. Mother's Day is coming soon, I must make some cards. I sell those too. Aunt Cynthia gave me the 52-color water gel markers. I have to do my menu, I draw tattoos and the kids pay me. Yeah! Mommy, it's fun. You see how much I made?" She counts $40.

I couldn't believe this little girl was getting her hustle on. I just couldn't believe it. So that Monday I picked her up from the after-school program. I didn't see her. I saw a bunch of kids surrounding a little girl who was on her knees and a line of kids had formed. The kids that were in the circle began to scream and jump, shouting, "That's nice! Oooo! I want that, I want mine like that." The little girl stood up and to my surprise it was Kola! I yelled, "Kola, come here, momma." She grabbed a folded sheet of construction paper that looked like a card. All the kids called her name and ran behind her. "Kola, do my tattoo!" She said, "I can't. My mom is here now. She had them tell her what they wanted. She gave them a booklet and they picked from the designs she had, or they would tell her to "do the one you did for this or that one." I could not believe my eyes. She said to one girl, "I am going to use brighter colors on you because it will be seen better."

All I could do was watch this little 10-year-old handle her little business. I remember Margaretta Young said to me, "She has an entrepreneurial mind. You got to do something with her; she is talented." It's amazing that this lady knew something I had no idea of. When her school uniform would get too small, she would make pocketbooks out of the material. The older sweaters she would cut the sleeves off and make leg warmers from them. She never ceased to amaze me. Oftentimes, I wondered how I was raising her without my mom. She had only one grandparent left—my Dad. Oh, how a grandmother would have loved having her as a grandchild. I think so much of the times when momma was alive, whenever she would get dressed, she would let Kola climb in her lap and go into the jewelry box my dad gave her back in 1949. Whatever Kola picked she wore. That was always precious to me and to her that her grandma respected her decision.

Even as a little child she had a mind to comprehend the importance of having clarity in her thoughts. I was reminded of when I came to pick her up from her afterschool program when she was in the 5th grade. She ran to me crying and shaking. "Mommy! The ants! The ants! I was twisting her and turning her, thinking ants were all over her. She handed me a notice and said a bunch of kids got suspended for leaving the playground, trying to run to the store and a teacher saw them and one of the kids almost got hit by a car. She said, "Mommy, I was with those kids and we were all running, then I remembered while I was running when I was 5 years old and we were at the bus stop. There were a bunch of ants you killed that day and one of them you didn't kill because you said it didn't follow the crowd. Mommy, it's true. I didn't follow the crowd and I am the one who didn't get in trouble." I held this little girl and I cried with her. She had no idea how much she validated me as a parent, giving her useful instruction that she was able to use and see the benefit of taking heed to.

What truly amazed me was a time while she was in junior high school. There was a handsome young fella who was her friend and she liked him a lot. This particular day this young man made her feel really bad. She and I were in the supermarket and she wasn't her cheery self that I am used to seeing. Kola loves food. For her to be a small-framed child, she eats a lot. So I studied her face and could see she was going to burst into tears at any moment. So I asked her what happened. She explained. So I told her ok, if you want to cry, go ahead and cry. Your feelings are hurt. She cried, and I hugged her right there in the middle of the supermarket.

So I pulled back from her and said, "Ok, so now that you've cried, what's next? Now if I were you, this is what I think I would do: I would go to school tomorrow, act like nothing happened. I would wait until everybody was together and when the boys started joking around, I would laugh really hard at all of their jokes. I would laugh uncontrollably. Then when he said something funny, I would make a point not to laugh at his joke. Another boy that said something after him, I would laugh uncontrollably. I would tell that boy he's mad funny. Tell him to say something else. It can be stupid. Laugh very heartily. Then when the boy that hurt your feelings tries to say something again, do like before. Don't laugh, don't say nothing. Act like he never said anything. I bet he's going to ask you what's wrong. Then you make a point to tell him exactly how he made you feel. She lit up like a Christmas tree. She was picturing it happening and she was also wondering if it would work.

We finished our shopping, got home and we were putting things away and preparing dinner, she was a real chatterbox. She said, "I thought you were going to be mad with me for crying over a boy." I told her, "No! You weren't crying over a boy, you were crying because a boy you like hurt your feelings. What he said to you,

you wouldn't have said that to him and your feelings were hurt. Also, because you like him, and you want him to like you like that. So that's what made it hurt so much." "Mommy, how'd you know? "Because your other friend said the same thing and it didn't bother you. Sometimes people you think wouldn't hurt your feelings might hurt your feelings. You have to be able to feel what you feel and then decide how you are going to handle them after." The looks she was giving me were, *I hope you're right, Momma.*

After we showered before bed and powdered, she came in my room. "Can I stay with you?" I said, "Sure." She went and made two bowls of ice cream and jumped on my bed, folded her legs eagle style and said, "Mommy, I really hope I can do it." I said, "Ok, let me show you. I'll be you, this is how you do it." She paid close attention, then she copied me. Well, the next day she came to pick me up from work. She had balloons, one rose and a pizza slice. She said, "Mommy, Mommy it worked. After school he ran to me, asked what was wrong, why I wasn't talking with him but talked with everybody else? He said, 'I will walk with you.' and bought me things. I told him friends don't turn on friends just because you find new friends. He said he was sorry. Mommy, Mommy it really worked." "This just helped him to see what he really thought of you and it mattered to him what you thought of him. Now you got to see what hurt feels like coming from someone you care about and that it's ok to cry, but you don't stay crying. It's healthy to let your tears out." I can remember the old school generation would tell a child or pre-teen, "Feelings can't get hurt," and wouldn't let them cry about it. I couldn't fathom telling my mom about a boy hurting my feelings. "Kola, it's important to be able to be in touch with your feelings. You are entitled to your feelings, but you must always ask yourself, 'What am I going to do with them?' Are you going to acknowledge it and make a choice to let those feelings bring about something positive, or let those feelings lead you somewhere negative?

"September 23, 1998 about seven years ago, your mommy was hurting really bad." Your Grandma had died in 1997 and Aunt Robin in 1998 and I was feeling angry with the world. You were with your dad on this particular weekend and I was letting my feelings get the best of me. Your uncle Jeffrey told me, "Tray, I am coming to pick you up and take you with me to Archie's church." I said, "Nah! I am not going there. I go to Rico church from time to time." Your uncle insisted. He said, "Tray, I don't know about no Rico, but I'm telling you Archie McInnis is the real deal. Archie is even married and got kids. His wife is good people. I went to his Installation Service when they made him a Pastor. He opened the church in his house in the basement, but it's a real church. You used to always sing Gospel music and read the children's bible. Come on. You can even bring Kola when she's not with Kevin. I'm coming for you from the Bronx to take you there. You know how I am, and I am telling you it's the real deal."

  Your uncle picked me up and we got there, but before I went inside, I smoked my cigarette. I wore a powder blue mini-skirt, white silk blouse, heels, long earrings and an attitude. I went down the stairs, I believe there was a sign that said Full Effect Gospel Ministries. Temporary location. Inside there were about 26 folding chairs neatly lined-up. The whole side of the wall was mirrored; there was a folding table with a white cloth and a crystal pitcher with ice water, a few plastic cups and two wine glasses, and also a pack of white handkerchiefs stacked neatly on this little table. There was a wooden podium in the center of the room facing the chairs. The keyboard and swivel chair were by the left side of the podium by the mirror, on the right side of the podium was a set of drums. There was a microphone on the podium and two stands with microphones. There were color printed programs on all of the chairs. Pastor Archie was on the keyboard, Brother Larry Morgan was on the drums. First Lady Cynthia and Brother Michael Wallace and Sister Marion Calendar were singing into the microphones. Brother Shareef Robinson read the program.

I remember the First Lady wearing a hat and was dressed beautifully. Their daughter Chelsea had on a fluffy dress, ruffled socks and the two little boys, Tre' and Aaron had on suits. Everybody was dressed very nicely as if they were at a real church building. My brother had on a suit and I felt out of place. My brother said it was in a basement, so I thought it wasn't going to look or feel like a church. I didn't know what I had just walked into, but I felt like I wasn't supposed to be there. Whatever Pastor Archie was going to say, I really didn't want to hear it. I wanted to walk out because I felt so out of place, and I knew if I left, my brother would keep asking me to come back. So I just stayed.

Well before I knew it, Pastor Archie started preaching and it seemed like everything I had hid down in my heart he knew. He spoke to my pain, like he knew what I was experiencing. I cried uncontrollably like I had years of tears. The floodgate was open and I couldn't stop crying. Service was over, and I was speaking to them and I was still crying. His wife First Lady Cynthia said to me, "There is nothing better than having a good cry. You're going to be alright, Sister Tracey." I also remembered Pastor Archie asking if anyone wanted to join the church. I said right then and there, "I would like to join. I have a six-year-old daughter who goes with her dad every other weekend. She will be here with me too." First Lady Cynthia said, "She is the same age as our daughter." Pastor Archie said, "I will be the best pastor you ever had." First Lady Cynthia hugged me, and the warmth of understanding was incredible. She said, "You're going to be alright." She said it with such certainty, like she already saw me better, when I didn't know what just happened. I just knew I would never be the same. I didn't know why I felt that or how it was going to happen; I just knew it.

Marion said, "You're not alone. We're here with you. Bring your little girl back with you." Michael said, "Hey Sister Tracey, this is the real deal like your brother Jeff said. I work with Pastor Archie in sanitation. Welcome to Full Effect. I know that when I left there my life changed completely up to this present day. Pastor Archie, now Bishop McInnis lives up to his words. That one decision changed the course of our lives. I was succumbing to my feelings in a negative way, but I made a decision and accepted Jesus in my life and made the choice to allow the change. It was a process and still is. So many times I wonder what life would have been like if I hadn't let Jesus be my Lord and Savior. What if your Uncle Jeffrey hadn't come for me? Kola, no matter what happens as you grow up, always choose God. I don't know what the process will be for you, but remember God."

Kola said, "You know what, Mommy? I remember when you were hurting. I remember during the time later on that I didn't want you to be alone. That's why when I was little I was hoping you would marry Poppy (Lonzel), when you started dating him. Daddy was getting ready to marry Janet and I wanted someone to marry you. I was going on 7 and I remember Poppy being with us all the time. He was like a father to me. He picked me up from school and then we would pick you up from work. He would cook, clean and help you with laundry. I saw you happy. He would pick us up early and make breakfast and pray before we'd leave for church. He would let me pray. He would ask you to pray and you would be scared and tell him you didn't know how to pray. He'd say, "Baby girl, tell your momma to just talk to God like she talks to us."

"Mommy, you know why I wanted you with Poppy? It's because when you were sick and I was with Daddy, he took care of you and he would speak to me every time. When I would call, he would say he was taking care of you. I never forgot that. Even Pop-Pop loved Lonzel; when he would cut his hair they would talk about the foods they like to cook.

"So Ma, since we talking, I am teenager now, can I go to the movies on my own with a boy?" "I am not ready to release you like that yet, baby girl. I have to go with you and the boy. I can sit a few rows behind you. The both of you can walk ahead of me. We can go eat. I'll sit at a different table. We can even go to Coney Island, so you two can get on rides and I will wait. I can go and play in the game room and you can come check on me every half hour. For you to go without me and just your young friends… not yet. "Oh, Mommy really? Thank you." "Now you can tell your friends you went to the movies with a boy. They don't have to know I was with you. Baby girl… Mommy will always be fair and true with you. Just remember sometimes you may hear me say no because… I have to be ready. It's just you and me; it gets scary sometimes. I have to know how to be your mom at the same time, be your sister and your friend. I'd rather be all those things first, so you can trust me over anybody."

An Unbreakable Bond

"Mommy (Kola was laughing hard, real silly right now). Mommy, do you remember when I was five and you asked me if I knew any curse words? You asked me to say them. So I said, 'A**.' You said, 'That's it? You don't know any other bad words?' I said, 'I know more. You said, 'Ok, say all of them and tell me when you're finished.' I said, 'Ok!' I was happy you were letting me cuss. So I said, 'A**, b***h, mother f***, s**t, d**n. That's it, Mommy, I don't know any more. Mommy, are there any more cuss words? You said, 'Baby girl, do you know those are all bad words? Do you know those are curse words?' I said, 'Yes, Mommy I know.' (And I was smiling from ear to ear because I got to say all the bad words). Then you said, 'Come close to me, Baby girl,' When I got within arms' length, you grabbed my face and squeezed my lips together. You screamed in my face and threatened me. You said, 'I better not ever catch you saying those words because now I know you know those are bad words and you don't have no business saying them. Kola, I better not ever hear anybody, I mean nobody, should tell me they heard you saying bad words.'

"Oooh, Mommy! I was so scared. I didn't know what just happened. I stopped smiling real fast. I knew I wasn't going to be saying those words. The funny thing was, I thought you were my friend when you told me I could say them. You tricked me, Mommy." "Kola, no I didn't trick you. I was being Mommy and letting you know early you weren't going to have a foul mouth. It was important to me that you knew it wasn't ok. The reason it was so important was because I let you be with your Aunt Cynthia, you was about 2 yrs old then. She would get upset with Montrice and say, 'I'm going to beat your ass, Montrice, if you keep misbehaving.' Now you could barely talk clearly.

One day we were visiting at my daddy and momma's house, you said to me in your little baby voice, 'Mommy, I bee at you rast.' I didn't know what you were saying. I was just smiling. I said, 'Mommy, look at Kola; she just talking up a storm and moving her head side to side and shaking her hip like she knows she's saying something. Pop-Pop said, 'She *is* saying something, and I know what she said.' I said, 'Daddy, what'd she just say?' He said, 'Tracey, ask her again.' I bent down smiling and excited my baby was talking. I said, 'What you say, lil momma?' She shook her head side to side, shook her little hips and this time pointed her little finger and said, 'Mommy, I bee your rast.' I was just a smiling. I said, 'I don't get what she's saying.' Daddy said, 'Tracey, she said, 'Mommy, I beat you're a**.' I know you're not supposed to laugh, but we cracked our sides laughing. I could not believe this little girl could come home to me and tell me she's going to beat my a**. My mother said, 'She done been over there at Cynthia's house and you know Cynthia will curse in a minute and tell Montrice that all the time when she gets in trouble. Call Cynthia and see if she told Montrice that she's going to beat her a**.'

"Well, when I called your Aunt Cynthia and asked her if she said that to you, she said, 'Yes, I did 'cause your pumpkin don't listen when I tell her something.' I said, 'Well your niece Kola's over here at Momma's house telling me she's going to beat my you know what. I didn't know what she was saying, but Daddy did.' Now your Aunt Cynthia was laughing so hard. She said, that's Auntie baby.' I said, 'Please try not to curse around her. She's still learning how to talk; I don't want the words she learns to speak clearly to be curse words. You know she adores. Do whatever you say she is going to repeat it. Wow, Mommy that was funny. Well, there are so many things you taught me when I was young that I still use now, and I am glad about it. So much I remember! Lots and lots of memories."

Chapter Eight

Who is this Child?
"Teenager"

"Kola, hurry up! Ms. Susan just called to say she will be here in 10 minutes to drop off the gift basket for First Lady Cynthia McInnis' Appreciation Service." She made sure to put all the items First Lady ordered from her Mary Kay products, plus she put extra stuff in there. I know Susan hooked it up. She loves our First Lady. I don't know why she hasn't joined Full Effect yet. She's been with us since the basement and comes to every major function.

"Kola, you hear me talking to you? Say something. You act like I'm talking to myself. Hurry up and run downstairs and meet her at the corner. She can't double park in front of the building. If you leave now, you will be meeting with her at the corner and she won't have to wait. I'm going to jump in the shower. By the time you come back, I should be getting out the shower. The warm water coming out of that new shower head is amazing." My sister Cynthia always knows where to get good stuff for a bargain or will find a way to get an item for the price she wants. Some people have that gift. After drying I stick my head out the door screaming, "Kola, Kola did you—" She screamed back at me with such an attitude that I could hear the sassiness. "Ma, I didn't go yet. I have to do my hair first. Ms. Susan isn't there yet anyways. The last time I waited 10 minutes for her."

I couldn't dry myself fast enough. I know this little girl did not sass me. I know she didn't deliberately not do what I asked of her. Who does this teenager think she is? "Are you kidding me, Kola? You mean you're *taking your time* to do what I asked you to do? You got the nerve to tell me you got to fix your hair first. When I was your age, picture me telling my mom or dad I'm not doing something they told me to do because I got to fix my hair. Anytime my parents told us to do something, we never made our parents wait. Who the hell you think you are to say that to me? Ms. Susan is a grown woman and you are a child; if you have to wait for her, you wait. She is a grown-up. You better take yourself down those stairs before I come out this bathroom and make you. I hate getting into it with you before we go to church. You better fix your attitude. You better check yourself."

The moment I stepped out the door, she left and slammed my house door. Aww man, this girl doesn't know I will knock her out. Wait until she gets back. Exactly five minutes after she left, Susan called to say she was just now leaving. I said, "Kola just left five minutes ago." "Oh good, I didn't want her standing out by the corner." This girl is so lucky. She don't even know that Ms. Susan just saved her from the quick beat-down I was about to give her. She don't realize I been paying attention to her. I noticed she been getting real sassy. She been saying, "Mommy look, I'm getting big as you." I don't know why she keeps telling me that. I know she ain't thinking about trying me. I got something for this little lady. All I can think about is as much as you love your children, you have to stay one move ahead or up on them. Especially with teenagers.

When I think of all the ladies in my world who had teenage daughters before me, I didn't quite understand some of the experiences they were having at that time. Kola was about 3 to 6 years younger than some of these teenagers. The one thing I can remember was all of these moms to these teenagers would say to me, "Sister Tracey, I know you love these girls and you're the President of the Youth Department, but their attitudes and sassiness… you better talk to them. I had heard it from all those teenage girls' moms. Loretta Johnson (Shaniequa), Audrey Ellington (Margaret), Paula Dye (Jasmine), Margaretta Young (Dominique), Denise Wade (Zarell) and Jacqueline White (Chenoa). These teenage girls' mothers were not missing a beat. I just thought they were the most respectful, talented, anointed, pretty young ladies. The young boys told me they came to our church because the pretty girls were at Full Effect. Well I now understand what those moms were saying to me. You think they're cute and innocent, but at home it's a different story.

Kola's Godmother Paulette Elliott would say my godchild is sweet and smart. My godchild can stay with me and her godsister Janeece MacDonald (Tati) anytime. She would spoil Kola and give her whatever she wanted and swore Kola did no wrong. I tried to tell her, your sweet godchild is changing. Paulette was another one that would have the teenagers stay at her house for the weekend and some young adults would stay too. We would try to allow the teenagers to express themselves in ways they may not have been able to at home or in church. She showed inspirational movies that would also help them on a spiritual note. I just knew when my time would come, having a teenager would be smooth. I was so wrong. I am now experiencing teenage sassy. I have to figure this thing out. I always try not to forget when I was a teenager. Think back to how I was. But then I consider I had siblings, so my time was a lot different than hers. I always considered her being an only child, so I thought I'd prepare myself for the teenage years. I make sure she gets to be around families and see how things are in a house with a lot of family members. When she was younger, I let her stay with the Johnson Family: Loretta and Larry and their children Shadell, Shanasia, Jesse, Patice, Taquana and Larry (Seven). I can remember her excitement at seeing how you had to share, wait your turn for bathroom time, cook and help with younger siblings. This helped her appreciate being an only child, but she also learned from that how to conduct herself when at sleepovers. The times she would be at Gloria Williams' house aka as Nana to Shakeita, her granddaughter. She is also mom to Shvangela, Shamel and Vivian. At that time all the other young girls including Naquaisha (Denise Wade's baby daughter) they would hang out and go roller skating, bowling and all those places the young adults would take them. Latisha, Nephetia, Elaughn, and Kira. So to see this attitude now I got to check it.

So I'm just thinking I have to show this little lady. She is sweet most of the time. Does all her school work, stays on the honor roll, but something comes over her and she sasses me with her mouth. So I waited one day when she was happy and nonchalant and decided to have a pillow fight with her. She loved pillow fights. So we were slapping each other with these fluffy pillows; we were laughing and giggling, jumping on and off the bed. So I decided to seize the moment and give her a lesson. So every time I hit her with the pillow, she would fall back on the bed and bounce back up, then I would knock her back on the bed. She'd get up again and I would shove her harder. She would get up again, and I'd flip her, then I'd hold her just enough to feel the pressure; I wasn't letting her up.

She said, "Mommy, Mommy, what's the matter?" I let her up. She was looking wild eyed and scared. She didn't know what happened. I said, "What's the matter, I was too rough? I'm sorry. Mommy got carried away. I was only playing with you. Imagine what Mommy could do if she was really angry and you tried me like you wanted to fight me." I tell you...I think that was our last pillow fight and she never said again, "Mommy, I am getting big as you." Nevertheless, it didn't stop her from being sassy. Our deal was from the day she entered school, "You're in school for 8 hours. You should never ask me to help you with your homework or projects. If you pay attention in class, you will never have to ask me because your teacher will give you instructions to get the job done. It wouldn't be fair for me to ask you to help me with my job when you're not there. When I go to open school night and get your report card, I will know what you been doing."

So we got there and the teachers told me, "Kola is a smart girl. She does all her work, turns in all her assignments. We think she is a little hard on herself. She has her personal goals and if she doesn't meet them, she gets upset. We don't want our students to put that kind of pressure on themselves." I was so proud. Alright! My daughter has goals with her education. I kept smiling and saying, "Oh! Thank you. She is very responsible. She's always, since she was a little girl, taken school seriously, Ms. Hines." "Kola's academics are outstanding, but she is very sassy. It's disappointing." I said, "I understand because she sasses me at home." When I left that school I was steaming. We got home, and I stayed cool like nothing was wrong. I asked her as usual, "What do you want for dinner?" Of course her favorite: pork chops, mashed potatoes, peas and apple sauce, her cupcakes and milk. The whole time I was cooking I kept saying to myself, *I know this girl didn't embarrass me like this. How did she get the nerve to try the teacher like that? She knows she ain't got no business sassing no adults, let alone a teacher. Lord, this girl be up in your house praising and singing. She knows I don't like fresh children. Especially not going to have mine being known as a fresh kid.*

So we got through dinner. I said, "Kola, get your clothes out for tomorrow." She had a huge walk-in closet with French doors. When you opened them, you were unable to see anyone at the entrance of your room. I stood at the door, waiting for her to close the door. Before I realized it, I punched her on the side of her head. Screamed at her like a mad woman. "This is my final warning. You better never embarrass me like that *ever* again." She stumbled back in the closet, holding her head. I couldn't believe how hard I hit her. Scared myself. That was all the buildup of her sassing me that I must have unleashed. She said she really saw stars. She couldn't cry or scream. She was so in shock. She couldn't believe I hit her, and she didn't realize the power of the punch. She staggered and sat on her trunk to shake herself.

Well, I was afraid, saying, "Lord, please don't let me hurt and bruise my child, but I need you to show this little girl her momma can't take certain things from my child. Help me and help her!" Needless to say she was in the high school she wanted to be in and in Manhattan like she wanted. I came home from work and listened to the answering machine. Her math teacher left a message and said Kola was being disrespectful in his class. Said he would like to speak with me. Fortunately, it was one of those days I only had a half day at work. I remembered how I responded the last time. So, I decided oh, ok…enough is enough. I'm going to let her dad know his Little "G" ain't so little anymore and she has been very sassy. It's time he stepped up and disciplined her with me. A stern discipline. His had to match mine.

So I told him, "Come over. Let's do this together and let her know we mean business." He said, "Ok." So her Dad got to the house. Now he was 6' 2" still muscled, strong looking, but when it comes to his Little "G" he is a marshmallow, as she says. I told him, "Ok, when she comes in, we're both going to be stern looking. Our voices got to be hard and our words got to be forceful. Let me go first and you piggyback off me. This will hurt her feelings and she will understand." She came in and I said right off the bat, "Have a seat. I know you're surprised to see your dad here. I told him to come to keep me from hurting you. I got a call from your teacher saying you were disrespectful. After you finished your test you pulled out your magazine.

"He said you are his student that averages a 90 in his class. You participate in all class discussions, set a good example. So he was taken aback at how whenever you take a test and finish early, you think you can pull out your magazine and do what you want. He explained to you the instructions were to remain seated and keep your desk clear until *all* test takers are done. You were talking back, not waiting for everyone, then when you finished early, you read your magazine. Kola, who do you think you are that you don't have to follow the rules? Just because you're doing well in school don't mean somebody owes you something and they're supposed to take your crap. You do well because you're supposed to. Now that you're in the school you want to attend, you're going be disrespectful to the teacher? Well maybe I should put you in one of these local schools around here where the teachers don't care. "This is *not* how you behave if this is the place you say you want to be. Kevin, go ahead, talk to your daughter. This is such a shame and embarrassing.

Kevin stood up and said, "You're not going to get to this point and think you're going to put us through this." I was standing on the side looking from the kitchen, but could see in the living room. Kola was sitting on the couch sunken and defiant looking. I was steaming by now watching her. I wanted to yoke her up. I was like saying to myself, *that's good, Kevin, get her.* Kevin said, "Kola, the holidays are coming. Don't think you're going to be getting your way." *Ooo!* I was saying to myself, *Yes, Kevin, tell her.* I was so proud of him. He was being stern. Loving this teamwork. We are on the same page. Yes! I was nodding my head yes in agreement. I could see she was beginning to get a different look. I was starting to get happy! So I started to back him up.

He let his voice get a little louder. He stood directly in front of her and said, pointing his finger at her, pounding on his chest. "I'm your father. You're not going to be out here being disrespectful. This has to stop! You hear me, Kola? Your mother better not get another call. You better stop this right now! If I ever get a call from your mother about you being disrespectful,

I'm warning you right now. You better STOP it! I mean STOP it! Right this minute. You hear me? STOP it!" He hit his chest and said, "STOP it! Then he spelled it, hitting his chest S O T P! Well when he spelled it S O T P! Kola burst into laughter. I threw my hands up like Florida from Good Times and yelled, "D**n! D**n! D**n!" That discipline went right out the window. I got so angry. Now this man knows he is dyslexic and sees letters jumbled up, why would he even attempt to spell? All I could do was laugh.

Next thing I knew, we were all laughing uncontrollably. Then he decided to go food shopping, since he saw that there were items missing from the fridge that he thought should have been there. So we went to the supermarket and he got all kinds of items she specifically liked. He said, "Little G," you want this, you want that? You know what, Tray? I'm gonna cook one of her favorite meals and maybe we play a quick game of Trouble and 500." I threw my hands up! "I tell you, Kevin, that's some disciplining you did. Thank God she got it and understands that if she goes down this path,

Tracey Hines

I'm going to transfer her to a school that is used to kids acting up, disrespectful and fighting.

Chapter Nine

Unexpected Events
"Struggle to Begin"

"Ok! So here's the deal. I have exhausted all of our money. I can't seem to find a job because I don't have a degree. Kola, Momma has a lot of work experience and the money I used to make, these companies aren't trying to hire me. Pastor McInnis let me work at the church and paid weekly what I was getting paid at my job that I am no longer working. I got caught up in wanting to be in a secular work office. Oh, how I wish I had stayed, but who knows what's ahead. So, you know, we must leave this apartment. You're 16 now and we've been here 8 years. The landlady has a brand new Mercedes, children in private school and one in college. She needs a tenant who can pay. She's been good to us. She let Pop-Pop stay with you and me for a year while he waited to move in his senior citizen building. She even let your father stay with us for a year when he needed a place. She never asked for extra rent. So right now we have to go.

"It's been 3 months she didn't get anything from me. The unemployment ran out, public assistance only pays $215. Bi-weekly. Nobody's going to rent to us only; I need a roommate. I spoke with Shaniequa, she works with the Parks Department. Pastor told me to ask her, said she could use the comfort of having someone with her too. He said, "She respects you; it could work out." "Momma, whatever we need to do, it's going to be ok. I love Shaniequa. She takes good care of Naliyah and Nyree. She even tries to always do nice things for me. Mommy, I know we're going to be fine; you helped a lot of people and you've been good to the family. God got us. Please don't worry."

"Kola, I am so sorry you have to experience this. You are such a great kid. You turned 16 and you're an Honor Roll student. You sing on the Praise and Worship team. You Praise Dance. Participate in every church activity, you even go when I don't. You don't deserve to experience this struggle with me. I wanted to do something really nice for you, even Shaniequa wanted to try and plan a Sweet Sixteen. Had so many people who was so sure I was going to do something for you."

"Mommy, I never wanted a party. You and Daddy bought my laptop, took me out to eat and gave me money. I still have money left; I can give it to you. Mommy, please! Don't worry about me. It's ok. We're going to be fine."

"Kola, right now Mommy feels horrible. I just knew I was going to find a job making the money I used to make by now. The hardest part is I have to ask Pop-Pop for another $1000 when he just gave me $1000 last month. He's on a fixed income and yet he tells me he always wanted to be able to help us when we needed it. He also said that's why at Christmas he'd like to make sure he can give us all nice cash envelopes. He looks forward to that for his kids. Even the church has helped pay the rent on several occasions. I refuse to ask anymore. I can only imagine once the word is out I've been helped, then everybody will start asking."

"Mommy, please, please don't worry. We are going to be ok. It's going to be alright. I can give you carfare every week when I get paid from my afterschool job. You don't have to buy me new clothes, I know how to bargain shop and I go to the good thrift shops on Park Ave or the good neighborhoods in Manhattan and get really good expensive clothing very cheap. I know how to fix my clothes and do my own hair. You don't have to worry about me, just do whatever you need to do." "Baby girl, you and I have to stay in the same room and share the bed. I told Shaniequa she can take both rooms so the girls can have their little room. You and I can share. I hate this apartment, but we don't have time to find anything else." "Mommy, we have a place and it's ours. We can make it comfortable until you find something else. Don't worry, I just know we're going to be fine."

"Baby girl, this time Mommy is at a loss and I don't have nobody trying help us financially anymore." "That's because God wants to take care of us, Mommy." "Kola, if you say so." "Mommy, Lonzel was at the church. He said he been wanting to make sure you ok. He said you haven't been to church in months." "What? I make sure to show up at least on Pastoral Day if no other Sunday." I gave him our address and he said he's

An Unbreakable Bond

coming by." "Baby girl, if anybody ask you about me, tell them to call me. You don't have to explain anything to anybody. I don't know why everybody worry about me not being there." "Mommy, it's because we've been there from the beginning and people are used to seeing you there all the time. You were the pastor's secretary, church clerk, vice president of the pastoral team, president of the youth department, youth Sunday school teacher, New Members Class teacher and a minister. That's why people are concerned.

"Deacon Brian Wade told me you better call him. He said he calls you every day; you need to answer his calls. He said you acting up. "That's a spirit, you know better." "Kola, I don't want you telling anybody anything about me or about what's going on. Tell them to call me or come see me. Right now only Poppy comes to see me. He reads the Word to me. Buys us food, prays for me and calls every day. He comes every Sunday and picks us up for church and Nina Daniels makes sure we get home. She goes out her way and she lives all the way out in Long Island. Kola, don't do what I do. You just make sure you go to church and don't worry about me.

Mommy is burnt out and I am no good for anybody right now." "Well, Mommy, I think you need to talk to Pastor and First Lady. You know they care about you."

"They don't care about me anymore; I've become a liability when I should be an asset." Oh, Mommy don't talk like that. They love us, but we have a lot of members and you are supposed to be the one who helped and not one who needed a lot of help because you were there the longest and did everything. You just stopped being a help. Pastor and First Lady have a lot of things they're doing. Plus, First Lady has been sick a lot and she still has to do everything." "Well... I'm not trying to be all that. I don't have no help. They have each other. I'm on my own. So I have to stop and take care of myself; who else is going to take care of me?" "My daddy and Poppy will take care of you if you need them. They really care about you being okay." "Kola, you don't understand. Just remember, what I do right it's ok for you to follow. What I do wrong, make sure you don't follow."

Saturday, June 26, 2010 I was awakened by banging on the door. The neighbors were screaming at me and Kola and ready to fight. They had been trying to tell us Charles had fallen out and had a heart attack outside in front of the building. He was 45 years old. The ambulance came and took him to the local hospital, where he died a few minutes after. We were renting a room from Charles. He lived on the first floor of a nicely furnished apartment with a back yard. He saw the place where I was living with Shaniequa, and he said, "You and your daughter cannot stay in that dump. She needs to be in a better place. He moved our things to his house in a cab. He said, "Because your daughter is so respectful to be a teenager, I will rent the room to you for $200 a week, cable and buy your own food.

    I had been working as a Security Dispatcher at only $13 an hour. My check was already being garnished. I would be left with $30 every week, just enough for carfare. When Kola and I got to the hospital, we saw his mother and girlfriend. They had pronounced him dead, but I went behind the curtain to try to conduct my own CPR and pray in the name of Jesus. I prayed so loud asking the same God that raised Lazarus to raise Charles. The God that breathed life back into the

Shunamite woman's son to breathe life back into Charles. The God that awakened the dead boy out of the box coming from the city of Nain to awaken Charles. Oh! God of Abraham, Isaac and Jacob, show yourself strong and mighty. My God, I know you always hear our prayer. Because they that stand around are watching, I need you to bring Charles back to life." Everybody in the ER area stopped. You could hear a pin drop. Charles' girlfriend Sharon said the way I prayed, everybody was waiting to see if he would come back to life. She was so sure. She said if he would have gotten up that whole ER would have got saved. She said Charles always said, "That Tracey is powerful. She only messed up right now because she doesn't focus; she gets distracted. If she ever gets focus she will be a real force."

Kola was devastated by the passing of Charles, (Pops). Sharon, me, Charles and Lonzel (Poppy) would be up all night playing spades and talking trash. Kola would come home and go get ready for bed. She would say, "Pops," and they both would answer. She was their daughter. The love and respect she gave them, they had never experienced that with anyone. So they would always say how blessed Kevin was to have a daughter like her. Even Sharon was impressed. Christmas of 2009 Kola bought gifts for everybody with her check. She wrote special notes to accompany the gifts. She even bought a gift for the cat that acted like a dog. They were all blown away. They all cried.

I remember Charles' reaction vividly. He told everybody and showed everybody that she bought him a diamond watch and said one day she will be rich and famous. She remembered Sharon loved purple and bought her a purple makeup case and Victoria Secret perfume that she loved. She bought Poppy a hat that he loved. She went all out for me: boots, clothes and a jacket. She saved her paychecks to bless us. Charles said, "Hey Tracey, where you get her from? She looks like her father and I guess she got his ways. 'Cause you, Tracey, you can be nothing but trouble. You got to do s**t your way. Every second or third word from Charles was a curse. He had a bad mouth but a heart of gold. Always willing to help somebody, but would fuss the whole time. Nobody better not tell him he couldn't help. He wanted so much for Kola to sing and model. He would promote her singing. He would help match her outfits and bags. They had a strong bond. He would make sure that Kola had whatever she wanted to eat. He was fascinated by how she was so little and ate so much and didn't gain any weight. After he died we could feel his presence with us. Like there was a scent that reminded us of him.

A month later Kola and I checked ourselves into the shelter system. We stayed there for three days. For the first time of all our going through one set of trouble after another, Kola said, "Mommy, I can't do this shelter living." "I told her, "You don't have to." She had graduated with her Regents Diploma. She always wanted to go away to college and her guidance counselors were fighting for her to go. She opted out and told me she couldn't leave me and go away to college, knowing she didn't know where I would be living. She said she wouldn't be no good, so she said, "I'm going to Empire Hair School and get my license." I couldn't believe she was making that sacrifice and she didn't have to. So I told Jazz, and Jazz allowed us to stay with her as long as we needed to. She was upset that I never told her all that we experienced. We stayed for a month and then we moved into our brand new apartment where we are still tenants.

Although we found ourselves in our own permanent housing, on Kola's 21st birthday, we found ourselves in housing court. I couldn't keep up with paying rent on time and they took me to court. It was so bad that I contacted Homebase and they helped with rent arrears. They set me up with an appointment. I picked up the letter, but it was getting too late to go to housing court. The City Marshal's office said they were coming at 2 p.m. to padlock my apartment. I finally had a horrible melt down on Kola's birthday. She grabbed me by both hands and she said the sweetest short prayer with confidence that I ever heard. I'll always remember this one because I was having the worst breakdown of my entire life and everything that happened from years before came racing through my mind. She said, "God, it's me, Kola. My mom and I need you. She doesn't know what to do and I don't know what to do. We need your help. Thank you for hearing our prayer. Thank you for helping us. All things whatsoever you ask in prayer believe it and you shall receive it. We receive what we believe, we have what we believe, and we are what we believe. Come, Mommy, bring your overnight bag and I have mine. Let's go to the housing court and give the letter to the judge like you were told. The whole time I was sitting there with tears coming down my face, saying to myself, *Not again, not again. I cannot do this. It's my baby's 21st birthday. She should be celebrated. She is an awesome kid. I am a horrible mother to let her experience this again. God, I need to pack up and go anywhere away from her. I am ruining her life. There is no way I can make up for the misfortunes and struggles she's had to endure.* "Mommy, wipe your face. Stop crying. It's ok. We're going to be alright."

"Respondent Tracey Hines, approach the bench." "Your Honor, I received this letter from a local agency. I need more time; they will work with me along with a few other agencies in the city. The City Marshals are padlocking my door today." He made a phone call, then said, "Come back a month from today; we should have some help or more time. We need to go do a show cause." "Thank you, your honor. Today is my daughter's

An Unbreakable Bond

birthday, her 21st birthday." "Happy birthday, young lady. Go home and enjoy your birthday. You have time now to get everything together." Kola said, "Thank you. God bless you." When we got home our building super came upstairs to me. He said, "The Marshals came to padlock your door. I told him, "I didn't know she had troubles. She and her daughter are good peoples." We were getting ready to put the key in the door when the judge called and said, "The case is stayed. She's been granted time." The super said, "I never seen anything like that before." When I opened the door he saw the birthday cake. He asked, 'Whose birthday?' Kola answered, "It's my birthday."

'Well enjoy your birthday.' He said to me, 'She's a good girl, she never gave you problems, I can tell. God wasn't going to let her down.' I told him she prayed the sweetest prayer. I knew if for no other reason, God blessed me because of her.

Chapter Ten

A New Beginning
"Keeping Our Legacy Alive"

On November 7th, 2015, the day was gray and dreary looking. Even though the sun wasn't shining it was fairly warm for November. Everyone that was in the apartment on that day hearts were full and shining bright.

This was the day of every mother's dream. My baby girl, Kola, was getting married to Ryan Roberts, a young man who is destined for greatness. He provides and brings my daughter happiness and joy. They are an unstoppable unit.

As Kola's father, Kevin, Ryan's mother Faith and I, began to help her get dress in her wedding gown, my heart filled with so much joy. As we each found a s a button to latch on her dress, the photographer captured every precious moment. We stood in amazement. She looked so beautiful.

I could only stand there and look on her with a prayer in my heart. I prayed that all the hardships she experienced with me, she will never have to experience ever again. Watching her move about my heart began to flutter and tears filled the back of my eyes. I had flashing memories of the day I gave birth to her and all the years from that moment to now.

Kola was ready and she began to give orders. "Let's go. I am ready."

She was ready on time. She was ready to get to the church. Most brides are strategically late. She was ready on time. We had to tell her to give the people time to fill up the church. She was ready to start this next chapter in her life.

It's amazing how when you begin to reflect everything comes flooding back as if it was yesterday. As we prepared for the wedding, from the selection of the bridal party, Bachelorette Party and actual wedding day, something stuck out at me. Two people that I hold very dear said something to me that I will cherish forever.

My sister Cynthia Brewster said to me, "Sis I am proud of you. My niece…you raised her well. You raised her up in the church. She graduated High School and is in college at BMCC. She's getting married to a man who has never been married and neither of them have children. She is doing it the right way."

The other person was her youth pastor, Shamel Freeland. She said, "Minister Hines you've done well. Kola represents your parenting. What we see with a child tells us about your parenting. Elder Freeland and I would like to buy her wedding cake." We told them the price and they bought it." I am forever indebted to both of them.

Kola and Ryan had marriage counseling and received blessings from our Bishop. They prepared their celebration within three months after being together for three years. The beauty in all of this is that Kola was marrying Ryan, whom she met through me.

As we entered the stretch Hummer, we began our route to the church. The videographer asked if there was anything I'd like to say. All of the bridesmaids sang in unison along with me, "My baby's getting married!" I constantly said this through their engagement.

That twenty minute ride to the church seemed like forever. I could only give thanks to God for giving

An Unbreakable Bond

me another chance to see His goodness. I was once again active in ministry, going forward in the things of God and believing in His Word completely. I could see the handwriting of God. He was aligning things in my life.

As we entered the church, it was standing room only. I entered the place like I was Ms. America waving my hand at the outpour of love being displayed. Her father and I sat in the front pew with tears streaming down our faces.

We watched them join hands in marriage by our Bishop Archie L. McInnis, II at our church Full Effect Gospel Ministries and it was filled with people, some standing.

My heart was filled with thankfulness. You can watch this beautiful union on my website. After two years of marriage they had a beautiful little boy, Ryan II, my first grandchild. He has brought us joy.

As Kola continues to be a great wife and mother, they plan to expand their family soon. The legacy will continue to grow.

It is amazing how our bond started as me being the one who gave her life and now I am being given a life because of her. Our unbreakable mother-daughter bond is the key to "**K**eeping **O**ur **L**egacy **A**live".

About the Author

Tracey Hines is an author, motivational speaker and entrepreneur. She is the founder of *Keeping Our Legacy Alive*, where her mission is to empower Mothers and Daughters to better their relationship from primary years throughout adulthood.

She teaches courses for mothers and daughters; Strategic Parenting, Developing Communication Model, Nurturing Loving Relationships and more. She is dedicated to improving family relationships through Mother and Daughter bonds, starting from the nurturing and developmental stages from the womb.

She is the author of *An Unbreakable Bond, The Ultimate Mother and Daughter Relationship*. Her upcoming books include, *"Kola's Island"*, a children's book and a 120-day daily empowerment book entitled, *"Setting the Tone – Write it, Speak it, See it"*

Tracey Hines is a licensed Minister and serves faithfully at Full Effect Gospel Ministries under the leadership of Bishop Archie L. McInnis, II, Senior Pastor and Lady Dr. Cynthia McInnis

www.ingramcontent.com/pod-product-compliance
Lightning Source LLC
LaVergne TN
LVHW041546070426
835507LV00011B/960